The Case of the Vanishing Video Camera

by Sunita Apte
illustrated by Scott Brooks

Harcourt
SCHOOL PUBLISHERS

Printed in the United States of America

ISBN 10: 0-15-351088-9
ISBN 13: 978-0-15-351088-5

Ordering Options
ISBN 10: 0-15-3510603-2 (Grade 6 On-Level Collection)
ISBN 13: 978-0-15-3510603-1 (Grade 6 On-Level Collection)
ISBN 10: 0-15-357984-6 (package of 5)
ISBN 13: 978-0-15-357984-4 (package of 5)

1 2 3 4 5 6 7 8 9 10 179 12 11 10 09 08 07 06

CHARACTERS

Narrator

Westlake Film Club Members

Sally

Rob

Wanda

Jason

Madison

Grace
Westlake
student

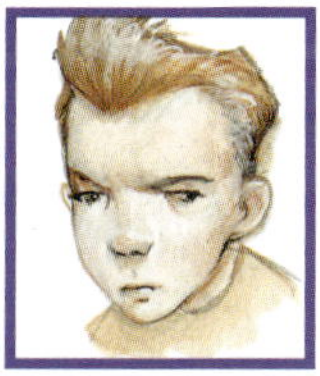

Tom
Westlake
student

Assistant
Principal
Hammond

Setting: The film studio at Westlake Middle School

Narrator: It's Tuesday, lunchtime. The Westlake Film Club has a big problem, so a special meeting has been called.

Sally: What are we going to do about this?

Rob: I don't know what we're going to do. All I know is that I'm going to be in big trouble.

Wanda: Maybe your mom will understand.

Rob: Do you think your mom would understand if her expensive digital video camera were stolen?!

Jason: Rob, calm down—let's not go haywire.

Madison: I know! Let's try to track down the culprit and get the camera back!

Rob: That's a great idea, but how do we start?

Wanda: Well, first, let's go over exactly what happened. You put the camera in your locker and then went to homeroom, right?

Sally: When you came back after first period, your locker was open and the camera was gone, right?

Rob: Right.

Jason: Did you lock your locker before homeroom?

Rob: I'm sure I did. I never leave my locker open.

Madison: Let's check around to see whether anyone was late for homeroom this morning. If anyone was late, then we have our thief.

Jason: What if more than one person was late?

Wanda: Then we'll look for the person who doesn't have an alibi and can't tell us what they were doing at the time of the theft.

Sally: That's a great idea. Everyone, check the attendance sheet in your homerooms. Then let's rendezvous again after school.

Narrator: That afternoon, the Film Club meets again.

Jason: What information have we unearthed so far? What's the extent of our knowledge? Was anyone late for homeroom this morning?

Madison: Jennifer was late.

Rob: Tom was late as well.

Wanda: Grace was late, too.

Sally: Okay, we have three suspects. Let's confront them tomorrow to see which one doesn't have a good reason for being late today.

Jason: That's a plan. Let's meet outside the cafeteria at lunchtime, and we'll do it then.

Narrator: The next day, at lunchtime, the club members wait outside the cafeteria.

Wanda: There's Grace. Let's ask her why she was late.

Narrator: The club members intercept Grace.

Rob: Hey, Grace, can we talk to you for a minute?

Grace: Sure. What's up?

Madison: We were just wondering why you were late for homeroom yesterday morning.

Grace: Umm, I woke up late and was late getting to school. Why do you want to know?

Jason: Someone stole Rob's video camera during homeroom yesterday. We figure that whoever it was must have come to homeroom late. You were late, so we were checking.

Grace: Tom was late, too. Plus, I saw him showing his friends a new video camera at lunch.

Sally: Aha! We've found our thief!

Wanda: Not so fast, Sally. Tom may have a perfectly good explanation for everything.

Rob: Well, I'd like to hear his justification for the fact that he has a new video camera the same day someone stole mine.

Madison: You can hear it now. Here he comes.

Narrator: The group stops Tom when he is about to go into the cafeteria.

Sally: Hi, Tom. We heard you got a new video camera.

Tom: Yeah, I got it for my birthday. Want to see it? It's in my locker.

Jason: Your birthday, huh? Was yesterday your birthday? Is that why you were late to homeroom?

Tom: Yes, it was. My parents gave me the camera in the morning. Then I stopped to do some filming outside school. I didn't realize the time, so I was late.

Wanda: Did anyone see you filming?

Tom: Yes, Jorge was with me. Why?

Rob: Someone stole my video camera out of my locker during homeroom yesterday. We were just checking.

Narrator: Tom's face turns red, and anger seems to seep from his pores.

Tom: Well, it wasn't me! My new camera came from my parents. It was a very special present!

Narrator: Tom stomps off angrily, and the group stares after him.

Madison: Do you think he's telling the truth?

Sally: I'm not convinced that we can rely on what he said. Let's ask Jorge and find out.

Jason: Well, I don't see Jorge or Jennifer, and I need to eat before lunchtime ends. Can someone track them down, and then we can meet again after school?

Wanda: Jorge is in my math class. I'll talk to him then.

Rob: I have art with Jennifer. I'll ask her why she was late to homeroom. Maybe she has an ordinary, good excuse.

Sally: Great! Let's meet in the film studio after school.

Narrator: That afternoon, the group gathers in the film studio.

Wanda: I talked to Jorge. He says he was with Tom when he was filming in the morning. He also said that Tom had been talking about getting a video camera for his birthday for months.

Madison: Hmm. Sounds like he might be telling the truth. I guess that's one theory rejected. Of course, I guess Jorge could always be lying for him.

Jason: What about Jennifer? Rob, did you talk to her?

Rob: I tried, but she wouldn't tell me why she was late. She said the information was confidential.

Wanda: That's suspicious.

Sally: Yeah, it sure is. Who would think that Jennifer was a thief? She seems like such an innocent person.

Madison: What a scandal. Jennifer, the sweet and talented, sinuous ballet dancer, is actually a thief.

Jason: Not so fast. I admit her behavior seems suspicious, but we don't actually know that she took the camera.

Wanda: I'll try talking to her tomorrow. Maybe she'll open up to me.

Narrator: Just then Assistant Principal Hammond barges into the studio.

Assistant Principal Hammond: Oh, excuse me! I didn't know anyone was in here. I just came to return this video camera.

Rob: My camera!

Assistant Principal Hammond: Oh, is this yours? A student found it in the cafeteria the other morning. I waited for someone to come and claim it, but no one did. Then I thought it might belong to the Film Club, so I decided I would bring it to the studio.

Rob: Thanks, Ms. Hammond. The camera belongs to my mother. She would have been very unhappy if I had lost it for good.

Sally: Well, I guess that settles it. The camera wasn't stolen after all.

Jason: Not so fast. Don't concede so quickly. Don't you wonder how the camera got into the cafeteria in the first place?

Narrator: Everyone looks at Rob. It makes him uncomfortable, and he smiles sheepishly.

Rob: I thought I put it safely in my locker.

Madison: I wonder who found it in the cafeteria.

Assistant Principal Hammond: It was Jennifer Johnson.

Wanda: Jennifer! Is there more to this story than meets the eye?

Rob: Do you think Jennifer may have stolen it and then accidentally left it in the cafeteria?

Assistant Principal Hammond: Jennifer Johnson does not strike me as a thief. She said she found it with the power on and still filming. Someone had just taken a movie following an ant crawling down the hallway into the cafeteria. When the morning bell rang, the person put the camera down.

Narrator: Rob looks as if he's just seen a ghost. Everyone stares at him.

Rob: I can't believe I forgot to put the camera away. I was so worried about getting to homeroom on time.

Assistant Principal Hammond: Well, I guess you kids won't be vying to solve this mystery anymore.

Narrator: Ms. Hammond leaves, and the club members turn to each other.

Madison: That must have been one interesting ant.

Narrator: Everyone nods and looks suspiciously at Rob.

Rob: *I* think we should make the ant the main subject of our next film.

Think Critically

1. What mystery is the Film Club trying to solve?
2. Who are the three suspects?
3. What are some adjectives you would use to describe the members of the Film Club?
4. Do you think the Film Club will be angry with Rob?
5. What would you do if something important to you was missing?

Social Studies

Film Directors Use the Internet or other library resources to find out about a famous filmmaker or director. You may want to find out about the director of your favorite movie. Write a few paragraphs about the person, including how the person got started in the business and how he or she gets ideas for films.

School-Home Connection Share the plot of this Readers' Theater with an adult at home. Discuss what could have happened next in the story.

Word Count: 1,332